# THE

# LITT

# RED

# BOOK

# OF

# FAMILY

# BUSINESS

**David Bork**

ISBN # 978-0-9637028-1-4

Published by

## SAMPSON PRESS

a division of
Coda Corporation

To purchase a copy of this book, please visit:
www.davidbork.com/redbook

For Mustafa Vehbi Koç

who knows the value
of "one good idea!"

## About David Bork

David Bork is one of the world's leaders in the field of family business counseling. Since 1968, he has served as an advisor to more than 400 families in business, re-shaping the course of history for those families and for the businesses they own. His keen insights and understanding of  complex cultural, business and family matters have contributed to his record of accomplishment as the consummate family business professional. He is a proponent of the Family Systems Approach to family business and pioneered the integration of Family Systems Theory with sound business practice.

Bork is the author of *Family Business, Risky Business – How To Make It Work*, and co-author of *Working With Family Business – A Guide for Professionals*, the first and only book of its kind in the field.

Bork has appeared on NBC's *Today Show* and been featured in *Fortune* magazine. He has been a regular resource for Young President's Organization (YPO) since 1984 and has spoken at many YPO Universities, including Venice, where he was named "Best of the Best," a designation for the most highly rated speakers. Since the late '80s he has had a concentration of clients in Turkey.

In 1998, the Family Firm Institute awarded Bork the coveted Richard Beckhard Practice Award, which recognizes outstanding contributions to the field of family business practice.

www.davidbork.com
970.927.8555
bork@davidbork.com

### Other books by David Bork:

*Family Business, Risky Business*
*– How to make it work*
  David Bork

*Working With Family Businesses*
*– A Guide for Professionals*
  David Bork, Dennis T. Jaffe, Sam H. Lane,
  Leslie Dashew, Quentin G. Heisler

*Handbook of Family Business*
*and Family Business Consultation*
*– A Global Perspective*

David Bork Authored Chapter 16:
"Family Businesses and Consultation to Them in Various Countries – Turkey"
David Bork Co-Authored Chapter 3: "The Aspen Family Business Group Consulting Process: A Model for Deep Structural Change and Relationship Shift in Complex Multi-generational Enterprising Family Systems"
Edited by Florence W. Kaslow, Ph.D.

For free articles and sample documents, visit: www.davidbork.com

Type: 'david bork' + 'family business' into your search engine for more choices of information.

## What Others Say About David Bork

"I like this book. You condense everything down to 280 points. This will be a handy reference guide and beacon for all who are connected with a family business. There is no question in my mind that David Bork played an important role in getting our family and our business to where we are today."

*Richard Kelley, Chairman of the Outrigger Hotels, Honolulu, HI*

"When my father became ill and died, David gave us the tools to manage the anxiety, uncertainty, and chaos that followed. Many in my family refer to the outcome as a true miracle. Today, we are healthy and strong with great opportunity."

*A. M. Clise, Chairman and CEO, Clise Properties, Inc., Seattle, WA*

"David Bork's keen intellect, straightforward manner and ability to clearly articulate his views made him an instant hit with our family. We did as he recommended, and our "100 Year Plan" has been the criteria we have used on countless decisions. "

*Bülent Eczacibasi, Chairman, Eczacibasi Holding, Istanbul, Turkey*

"David Bork's insight into our complex family dynamics and sensitivity to the needs and priorities of all family members made for a smooth transition between generations. Because of his professional manner and creative methodology, this was accomplished with both style and grace, something that would not have happened without him."

*Mustafa Koç, Chairman, Koç Holding, A.T.M.*

"David is very bright, compassionate and capable...a trusted advisor & friend. Our family is indebted to the advice and counsel from the great David Bork."

*Jack Mitchell, Chairman, Mitchells*

# TABLE OF CONTENTS

# i

# INTRODUCTION

I wish to convey the respect and admiration I hold for "my families" - the people I have served in my family business consulting practice since 1968. Together we worked, struggled, laughed and cried as we wrestled problems to the ground, resolved them, and got on with professionalizing their enterprises. I am humbled by their confidence and trust, inspired by their creativity and commitment to family business.

As a consultant in service to families who own businesses, I always thought I needed to be grounded in some sound set of theories. I still think that is important, but not once, never in 40 years, did someone in a family business say to me, "What is the theoretical foundation for that idea?"

Clients always wanted an unvarnished,

pragmatic solution. "What will work?"

Because of this, I learned to "practice the art of the possible." This book is about what works.

You won't find complex theories here, nor will you find everything about family business. This is a "little book," not a big one. What you will find are clear, common sense tips, advice and direction that will be useful in your family business. Implementation of even a few of these ideas is certain to decrease concerns about your family and your business and increase your contentment in life.

David Bork

**Notes:**

# 1

# ATTITUDE

**1.** One entrepreneur exclaimed, "My business is the most important business in the world! It keeps a roof over my head, feeds my family, educates my children, pays my country club dues and makes my wife happy. I am the luckiest man I know!" I think that entrepreneur was right.

**2.** If you regularly come home from work and exclaim, "Wow! I had a great day today," then go on to discuss what you did and why it was so interesting, challenging and stimulating for you, then everyone in your household will develop a positive attitude about what you do and where you do it. They might even want to help out. If, on the other hand, you regularly come home to grumble and complain about problems at work, family members might think you are a saint for going there every day, but they won't see it as a place they want to work. Be aware that wherever you go, you are teaching attitude.

**3.** The family business is important to its owners, but it must not become the metaphor for the family.

**4.** There must be some semblance of a family life that is not completely dominated by the family business.

**Notes:**_____

_____

_____

_____

_____

_____

_____

_____

# 2

## BUSINESS

**1.** Focus on profits, drive the top line and aggressively control costs.

**2.** If something is right for the business, the owners will benefit in the long run.

**3.** Keep the focus on the business! Its success is what makes other things possible. Don't be distracted by family matters.

**4.** If the business does not prosper, then the family will not be prosperous.

**5.** Serve your customers well, give them good value and they will keep coming back for more.

**6.** The cost of getting a new customer is much greater than the cost of keeping an existing one. In retail, this ratio is 7:1.

**7.** The best run companies have a commitment to provide a stable, predictable place of employment for employees. In return, the owners, who have capital at risk and reap the profits, can expect employees to give their best efforts.

## Notes:

_____

_____

_____

_____

_____

_____

_____

# 3

# BOUNDARIES

**1.** "Good fences make for good neighbors." - Robert Frost. When it comes to fences, there is one side and the other side. It is a boundary.

**2.** Boundaries determine how the family will interface with the business. Failure to define the interface between family and business is at the root of many family business problems. Family members must not meddle in areas for which they do not have responsibility.

**3.** When you define roles, responsibilities, accountability, ownership, owner and operator prerogatives, employee responsibility and private matters, you are creating boundaries.

**4.** Boundaries need constant maintenance if they are going to do the job for which they were intended.

**5.** A good rule; call it a boundary: "No discussion of family business at holiday dinners, birthday parties or _____." (You fill in the blank.) When you have this rule, or any other, observe it.

**6.** When your business is large enough to have non-family professionals leading divisions, and you have a board of directors, "No two hats" is a great policy. Being in a line position and on the board of directors is a conflict of interest and always presents complications.

**Notes:**_____

_____

_____

_____

_____

_____

_____

_____

# 4

# CHILDREN

## FUNDAMENTAL TASK OF PARENTS:

**RAISE RESPONSIBLE ADULTS
WHO HAVE HIGH SELF ESTEEM AND CAN
FUNCTION INDEPENDENTLY IN THIS WORLD.**

**1.** Give them unconditional love.

**2.** All activities that relate to preparing children for what lies ahead can fit into one or more of the three elements in the box above.

**3.** A united parental unit is essential to effective parenting.

**4.** Praise, encouragement and positive reinforcement are essential to building high self esteem in children.

**5.** Parents must teach their children useful problem solving skills, then get out of their way and let them use those skills.

**6.** Children need to be encouraged to solve their own problems. If parents try to "fix" everything for their children, they actually impede the child's development.

**7.** Life includes success and failure. Parents must help their children to learn from both.

**8.** Quality time – one parent with one child doing things of interest – is a wonderful time to build the relationship and listen to the child. If the parent listens, the child will share his/her concerns.

**9.** The attitudes of children are directly related to the relationships they have with their parents, the quality of those relationships, and the ability each has to listen to the other. Really listening and acknowledging the feelings behind what has been said creates and enhances the bond between individuals.

**10.** Do not compare one child with another. Each is his/her own unique individual.

**11.** Parents' expectations of their children need to be individualized for each child.

**12.** Teach your children that ownership of a company carries great responsibility.

**13.** Affluent parents must teach their children the relationship between effort and reward.

**14.** High-performing businessmen and businesswomen can accomplish many things. In their parent/child relationships, these performers often "suck the oxygen" out of the universe, leaving none for the child. This kind of parent must learn to take a lower profile in the relationship and avoid a know-it-all attitude, thus sharing control of the relationship with the child. Every child needs "oxygen."

**Notes:**_____

_____

_____

_____

_____

_____

_____

_____

# 5

# COMPENSATION

**1.** Pay fair market salaries to everyone. This is the way a person comes to understand their real value to the business and in the marketplace. This is a dose of reality.

**2.** If you want family members to receive more than fair market salary, call it the "family factor" or money from the "Lucky Sperm and Egg Fund," but don't call it a bonus for performance. It is a gift. Calling it a bonus creates an inflated view of contribution and self, which leads to arrogance and a sense of entitlement. Then you have a real problem.

**3.** Don't try to control your children with the purse strings. It keeps them in an adolescent position and they never grow up. (See Money)

## Notes:_____

_____

_____

_____

_____

_____

_____

_____

_____

# 6

# COMPETENCE

**1.** No business will be successful if the leadership is not competent.

**2.** Be honest with yourself when assessing your children's competence.

**3.** There is no correlation between the family gene pool and competence.

**4.** If a person is smart, they can pretend to be dumb, but a person who isn't smart cannot fake it.

**5.** The ability to sustain high level performance over time is the best evidence of competence. A "flash in the pan" performance is like the sizzle on a steak, gone in a moment while the odor lingers on.

**6.** If you employ a family member who is less than competent, they will not be able to perform at an acceptable level. They won't be asked to give input nor will they be given interesting things to do. Now you have created a business problem: you have an employee who is in the way and you have an unhappy family member. What a mess! Who is responsible for this mess? Who will clean it up? It is probably better not to make this mess in the first place.

**Notes:**_____

_____

_____

_____

_____

_____

_____

_____

# 7

# COMPETITION
# IN
# THE FAMILY

**1.** It is best when family members focus their competitive energy on competitors in the marketplace and not on each other.

**2.** Competition between siblings didn't work for Cain and Abel. (Bible: Genesis 4:1-16, Qur'an 5:26-32.) They were the first and second sons of Adam and Eve. Abel received approval for his actions. Cain was so jealous of Abel, he murdered him. It all started with sibling competition, then got out of hand.

**3.** When competition appears between family members in your business, nip it in the bud or it will undermine the business. If it doesn't stop, fire them both, then take them to a ball game and dinner. If they try to discuss the matter during the game or dinner, tell them you love them and there will be no more discussion of the matter.

**Notes:**_____

_____

_____

_____

_____

_____

_____

_____

# 8

# COMMUNICATIONS

**1.** Effective communication starts by being clear and constructive. Why would anyone wish to be unclear or destructive? Doesn't make sense. You might ask those around you for feedback on your communications. (See Feedback)

**2.** In a healthy business, vertical and horizontal communications in the organizational structure are relatively undistorted. One never has reason to question the veracity of information received from anyone else. If this doesn't characterize communication in your business, you need to hire a communications specialist to help you "make it right."

**3.** Never carry "the message" from one family member to another. The carrier risks getting caught in the middle, especially if there are differences between the sender and the intended receiver. If a family member asks you to "Tell X, ..." reply, "I understand your request. You will have to tell that to X yourself."

**Notes:**_____

_____

_____

_____

_____

_____

_____

_____

# 9

# CONSTITUTIONS
# CONDITIONS
# CONTRACTS

**1.** A family constitution and the U.S. constitution serve the same function. Both contain the ground rules for interaction, set the goals and define the conditions for how things will be done. Each has a methodology for resolution of differences. In family business, it defines the conditions of the interface between the family and the business.

**2.** Make a family constitution before you need one. If you don't have one, then now is the time to make one. If you are at the point where you really need one in order to manage conditions, terms, roles and relationships, it may be too late. In the latter case, the process of making your constitution will "smoke out" the real problems in your family. You may need professional help to get the agreement completed. (See Succession and Transfer of Control)

**3.** Convert the strong oral traditions of the family into written, binding agreements.

**4.** Differentiate between the task of family (See box under Children) and the task of business. The task of business is to make profits, and acceptance is conditional, based on the ability to produce and perform. Families who don't understand these differences will use the business as a vehicle to complete the family task. Families who confuse these two tasks create huge problems for themselves and others.

**5.** Include in your constitution that your intent is to operate the business in the most professional manner possible or according to International Best Practices for Family Business. This sets the standard for judging the way you operate or the way family members perform their jobs.

**6.** There must be a buy/sell agreement so that ownership shares are transferred in an orderly manner. This agreement must define the methodology for valuing the shares at the time of sale. In sales transactions, price is always an issue.

**Notes:** _____

_____

_____

_____

# 10

# DECISION MAKING

**1.** It is necessary to modify one's decision-making model to fit the decision to be made. One size does not fit all.

**2.** Certain decisions are best made using the consensus model with all family members involved, while other decisions are best made by one person or a smaller group. It all depends on the decision to be made.

**3.** In a healthy family business, decisions are made at the lowest level in the organizational structure where the responsibility for the outcome lies.

**4.** Upward delegation of decisions always creates a bottleneck. Bottlenecks lead to a backup of decisions, resulting in decisions not being made, details falling through the cracks and opportunities being lost.

**5.** Families often fall into the trap of having everyone in the family involved in making all decisions. This family pattern of involving everyone is symptomatic of a business that does not have clarity of roles, responsibility and accountability for different things. (See Boundaries.)

**6.** It is okay for everyone to have an opinion. It is not okay for everyone to think that their opinion should always prevail. The person who has the responsibility and will ultimately be held accountable should have the final say.

**7.** Criteria-based decision-making starts with defining the desired outcome, then listing the possible alternative actions, which may include doing nothing. You might begin by writing, "The desired outcome will _____." The next step is to list alternative actions to achieve this outcome and then make reasonable predictions for each of them. Finally, you select the alternative that will move you closest to the desired outcome in your written statement. This method reduces the personal ownership of the idea and lets the criteria make the choice.

**8.** An idea does not care who has it. The idea has no opinion on its inventor. Often in family business, the maker of an idea gets so attached to this idea that he/ she becomes blind to ideas presented by others. This quickly leads to polarization over whose idea is better, rather than which idea is better. This produces a new kind of problem, an ego problem.

**Notes:**_____

_____

_____

_____

_____

_____

_____

_____

# 11

## FEEDBACK

**1.** The word "feedback" came into our vocabulary in the '60s when the first satellite went into orbit. Information was sent from the satellite to a computer on earth, where it was processed, modified, and sent back to the satellite, which then corrected its trajectory as it moved through space.

**2.** Feedback, in the behavioral sense, is neutral information that describes observed action. Feedback can then be processed and considered. It may then lead to changes in behavior. With feedback, one obtains new information that may be useful in modifying one's behavior and becoming more effective. Try both evaluating feedback given to you and giving constructive feedback to others.

**3.** The difference between feedback on performance and criticism of performance is this: Feedback is neutral and descriptive, with the focus being the impact of the individual's behavior on the circumstance. "When you did this, I saw that happen." The intent is to point out details of behavior and their consequences so the individual can then consider and use this information to modify their behavior and perhaps change the outcome. Criticism always carries judgmental notions, focuses on what the individual did wrong and almost always precipitates defensiveness and alienation.

**Notes:**_____

_____

_____

_____

_____

_____

_____

_____

# 12

# FOUNDERS,
# THE
# VISIONARIES

**1.** God love 'em! If it weren't for founders – the visionaries who create businesses and want to share with their families their delight in their business – none of these problems would be present.

**2.** Some founders can be so controlling that it is pointless for family members to even consider working in the business.

**3.** The adage, "It is hard to find your place in the sun in the shade of the family tree," may be a reality in some families. If this is your reality, look for some sunshine away from the family tree or be satisfied with stunted growth.

**Notes:**_____

_____

_____

# 13

# GOVERNANCE

**1.** Governance establishes the rules of engagement and how the game will be played. It also defines boundaries. (see Boundaries) One family called it "The Family Deal." What is the deal in your family?

**2.** An advisory board, made up of outsiders who are not "cronies," is a good way to push the governance envelope. The board creates an environment where owners, in conjunction with third parties, can examine possibilities, suggestions and directions that they might not otherwise consider. Advisory Boards can add real value, especially when dealing with succession!

**3.** In your governance agreements, include a mechanism for binding resolution of disputes. It could be mediation, binding arbitration or some other process, so long as it gets disputes resolved. If you have a mechanism of this type, there is a good chance it will never be used. If you don't have it, sooner or later someone in your family will wish such an agreement existed. Think of the dispute resolution mechanism as insurance on your peace of mind or peace in your family, like the insurance on your life, home, automobile and other assets. What value do you place on peace of mind or peace in your family?

## Notes:_____

_____

_____

_____

_____

_____

_____

_____

# 14

## JOBS

**1.** Teaching a child to work, to carry a job to completion and know they have done the best they can do, are among the most important lessons of life. (See Children)

**2.** The ability to take a job and carry it through to successful completion brings satisfaction, enhances self esteem and builds a base for the next opportunity.

**3.** If a family member is to enter the family business and be successful in it, there must be a real job for him or her, and the skills to match the job.

**4.** Opportunity in the family business is not a birthright. It may be presented, but the right to seize it must be earned. (See Competence)

**5.** Create a family business employment policy so there is no question about conditions, terms, preparation, performance evaluation, entry and exit. The family business door must swing both ways, "In" and "Out." If it is possible to enter the family business, then it must also be possible to exit.

**6.** Any family members wishing to enter the business should be required to have three to five years experience working elsewhere, with the last job at least two years in length and involving one or more promotions. If your son or daughter didn't earn a promotion in the last two years of the job they held before coming into your business, then chances are he/she wasn't a great employee. If they are not a great employee for someone else, they won't be great for your business either.

**Notes:**

# 15

## KEYS TO IMPLEMENTING PRACTICES AND POLICIES

**1.** In family business, one can craft an elegant business solution, but the keys to implementation are always locked up in the family psychology. If you pay attention to the elegant solution and the family psychology, you will be more successful in your implementation rate, and your satisfaction quotient will be much higher.

**2.** Make a written timetable for implementation of the practice, policy or task, the date for completion and who is responsible and accountable for getting it done. Then, as time unfolds, ask that person how they are doing on the project and if they need any assistance, being careful not to sound like a nag. Your question opens the door for discussion of the project and can lead to an even better outcome for everyone. Be careful not to usurp responsibility for the project if you are not the responsible party.

**3.** Keep decisions about family business matters out of the parent's bedroom.

**Notes:**_____

_____

_____

_____

_____

_____

_____

_____

# 16

# MARKETING AND YOUR FAMILY BUSINESS

**1.** Marketing the fact that your business is family owned produces a positive response from most people.

**2.** The fact that a family has been in business for years suggests to customers that your business is one that people can trust.

**3.** If the family ownership is used in marketing, then it is important for all family members to practice the values the family claims to have.

**4.** Marketing the family ownership carries a risk. Don't confuse the boundary between the family and the business. You are simply using the ownership as a marketing tool. (See Boundaries)

**5.** The family ownership not withstanding, your product or service must be priced right, and it must do what you say it will do.

**Notes:**

# 17

# MONEY

**1.** Money is nice to have. It gives you choices.

**2.** If you have money, it becomes less important. If you don't have it, it looms large.

**3.** Money solves none of life's important problems. It can't make a sick baby well or bring back a dead parent.

**4.** Money is a tool, but should never be used as a hammer.

**5.** It is important for children to learn the relationship between effort and reward. Those who do not learn this lesson will have money problems at some point in life and will say there is never enough.

**6.** Money is complicated. If you "live large," and are thinking about giving your children enough to live the same way, you are playing with matches and gasoline. Let them learn to live within their means, on what they earn, plus - maybe - the family factor.

**7.** Children must learn to make do with what they have. Those who do not learn this, make doo doo. It smells.

**8.** Money should never be a disincentive to have a productive life.

**9.** Every business needs "dry powder," or cash reserves. In the early days of building a business it is hard to build a cash reserve, but if you are successful, there will come a time when building these reserves is possible.  Don't miss the chance to do it.


**Notes:**_____

_____

_____

_____

_____

_____

_____

# 18

## QUALITY

**1.** "The bitterness of poor quality is remembered long after the sweetness of low price is forgotten." – Anonymous

**2.** Sometimes "good enough" is good enough. There are moments, times and places where perfection is overrated! Knowing when to make this call and go for "good enough" comes from learning the lessons of life. This applies to nearly everything.

**Notes:** _____

_____

_____

_____

# 19

# RETIREMENT

**1.** It is not necessary to retire, but founders who don't plan to retire have an obligation to tell successors that is their plan. Don't say, "Someday this all will be yours," and know in your heart of hearts that "someday" is the day after your last breath. No secrets!

**2.** If founders do not retire in their mid 60s or by age 70, it is quite likely they will "die with their boots on."

**3.** The founder who does not fund his retirement as he goes along in business will stay and meddle because he must watch his money.

**4.** The founder who does not have hobbies

and interests outside of the business will be a problem for his successors.

**5.** There is a time and a season for everything. Knowing when to step aside and get out of the way is real wisdom.

**6.** The founder who thinks of his business as an extension of himself will have difficulty transferring the business to his children. He will stick around to protect his interests. Children are advised to duck!

**7.** There is more to life than family business. Repeat: There is more to life than family business.

**Notes:**_____

_____

_____

_____

_____

_____

_____

_____

# 20

## RICH

**1.** Sophie Tucker said, "I've been rich and I've been poor. Rich is better." Sophie had it right. (See Money)

**2.** Being rich is being able to live off the interest on your money. Really rich is living off the interest on your interest.

**3.** If you are rich, you must either manage your money, or manage the people who manage your money. If your children are rich or will be rich someday, teach them how to handle the burden of this responsibility. Ignore teaching them this lesson and rich becomes an accident waiting to happen.

**4.** The task of successors is to compound the family asset over the period of time that they are the stewards of that asset. That means that successors must think of those who will follow them.

**Notes:**_____

_____

_____

_____

_____

_____

_____

_____

# 21

## SELLING THE FAMILY BUSINESS

**1.** Emotional attachment to the family business can cloud your thinking. If one of your ancestors founded the business, give them credit for doing so and for giving you the opportunity you have had, but don't feel obliged to make any decision on the basis of what they might or might not have done.

**2.** You have to make today's decisions, not your ancestor who founded the business. Today is a different time with different conditions and variables to consider. Think as Bill Wrigley, Jr. did when he sold his great-great grandfather's company, "We must respect the past but do what's right for the future." In April 2008 he sold The Wrigley Company to Mars, founded in 1911 by Frank Mars and still owned by his descendants.

**3.** A family business should be treated like any other asset. When you make an investment, your motive is to maximize your return from that investment. The same applies to family businesses.

**4.** Selling the family business can be about wealth creation.

**5.** There is a time to buy and a time to sell. Timing is everything.

**6.** If and when you sell, set some of the proceeds from the sale aside. Call it "dry powder," your "reserves" or your "rainy day fund."

**7.** Selling part of your business is an option. Taking on a minority partner can be a liquidity event for the family or provide funds for needed expansion. Be aware that a partial sale will introduce a new dynamic into the governance of your business.

**8.** Redeploying some or all of the assets may be the best choice from your list of options when looking to compound the asset pool.

**Notes:**_____

_____

_____

_____

# 22

## SIBLING
## RELATIONSHIPS

**1.** Sibling relationships are not a problem if you are an only child! (See Competition)

**2.** Siblings will carry into the family business the problem solving methods they learned in the family. (See Children)

**3.** Teach children collaborative problem solving, and there's a chance they'll be friends for life.

**4.** Teach young children to have fun with each other. In that process, they'll learn to share power, a skill they will need if they are ever in business with one another.

**Notes:** _____

_____

_____

# 23

## SPOUSES

**1.** Some families make the rule that spouses may not work in the business. Families with this rule probably have good reasons.

**2.** In family business, it seems antithetical to create a structure that undermines the fundamental family unit, which is husband and wife. The question is not if information will be shared with spouses, but how much and in what way. Each family must make this determination for itself.

**3.** Spouses have a right to receive general knowledge about the family business and its stability. That is only fair. Spouses can have opinions about the business, but must recognize that only those in operating positions make and implement decisions, and it may be best to keep some opinions to themselves.

**4.** Private family information must remain private. Children must learn this at an early age.

**Notes:** _____

_____

_____

_____

_____

_____

_____

_____

_____

# 24

# SUCCESSION

**1.** Succession is when one individual or group of individuals passes complete control to someone else.

**2.** Involve the entire family in making the succession plan, making clear that the collective goal is for the business to survive, grow and prosper if the family is to benefit.

**3.** Succession is about continuity of the business as a viable economic unit, not who sits in the corner office. (It is possible that a non-family professional is the best person to sit there.)

**4.** Advisory boards provide third-party perspectives and can play an important role in vetting and implementing succession plans.

**5.** Succession begins long before the retirement party has been scheduled. Successors are taught to take responsibility at an early age, then are given more and more responsibility as they demonstrate proficiency in handling it. It starts with a job, then running a department, then a division and so on, until they are in charge of the entire business.

**6.** Successors must learn to watch the money. Failure of successors to really understand the financial aspects of keeping the business fiscally sound is a common cause of failure in family businesses.

**7.** The successor who is focused on "living well," and forgets about minding the store or feeding the goose that lays the "golden eggs," will ultimately dine on roast goose.

**Notes:**_____

_____

_____

_____

_____

_____

_____

_____

# 25

# TRANSFER
# OF CONTROL

**1.** There may be one somewhere, but I have never seen a founder who, in his heart of hearts, wanted to give up control of the business he founded. The business has been his lover, mistress, playground and best friend. It is hard to say "good bye."

**2.** If transfer of control doesn't happen by the time the founder is 65 or 70, then it isn't going to happen. That is OK only if the founder makes that clear to his successors.

**3.** In some families, transfer of control occurs only after prominent funerals. On the way home from the cemetery is the wrong time to be working out the details of succession and transfer of control. Game Over . . . for everyone!

## Notes:_____

_____

_____

_____

_____

_____

_____

_____

# 26

## TRUST

**1.** Trust among family members is the single most important element in mutually satisfying relationships. Without trust there is no mutual respect, and there will be no safety in the relationship for anyone.

**2.** Character is built one decision after another. It is important that each decision carry its own integrity.

**3.** Trust is built by doing what you say you will do, each and every time. A promise made is a debt unpaid.

**4.** When trust has been breached, it is very difficult, sometimes impossible, to reconstruct the relationship. Don't risk it.

**5.** Boundaries, governance and "The Family Deal" are all grounded in trust and designed to define expectations, reduce areas of potential conflict and increase the level of trust in the relationships. (See Boundaries and Governance.)

**Notes:**_____

_____

_____

_____

_____

_____

_____

_____

# 27

## WILLS
## TESTAMENTS
## BEQUESTS

**1.** Don't die without making one. It leaves a mess for someone else to clean up.

**2.** What is yours is yours to give to whomever you please.

**3.** Fair and mathematical equality are not the same.

**4.** If some of your children are in the business and some are not, give the business to the children who work there and other assets to those not in the business. The fundamental interests of the two groups will never be the same - ever - so don't set them up for conflict.

**5.** Don't try to legislate from "the other side." Nobody wants to see your bony hand pulling the strings.

## Notes: _____

_____

_____

_____

_____

_____

_____

_____

# 28

# 10 KEYS TO SUCCESS IN FAMILY BUSINESS

**1.** Shared values about people, work and money

**2.** Shared power – this does not mean equal power

**3.** Traditions – the glue that holds the family together

**4.** Willingness to learn and grow – this means the family is open to new ideas

**5.** Participation in non-business-related activities to maintain relationships

**6.** Genuine caring about one another that is expressed in overt actions

**7.** Mutual respect for one another that is grounded in trust

**8.** Assistance and support for one another, especially in times of grief, loss, pain and shame

**9.** Respect for one another's privacy

**10.** Well-defined interpersonal boundaries

This list was developed 20 years ago, based on my first 20 years serving family enterprise and what I saw happening that was described as "successful." It characterizes the families that remain "positively connected" in an economically viable business. It has been used as a template and workable set of criteria against which families can measure themselves.

For more information, see:
www.davidbork.com/articles/tenkeys.pdf

**Notes:**———————————————

——————————————————————

——————————————————————

——————————————————————

——————————————————————

TO PURCHASE OTHER DAVID BORK
BOOKS OR TO PURCHASE ADDITIONAL
COPIES OF THIS BOOK, PLEASE VISIT:
**www.davidbork.com/redbook**